Four Hours to Basic Japanese

Kiso Nihongo Yo Jikan

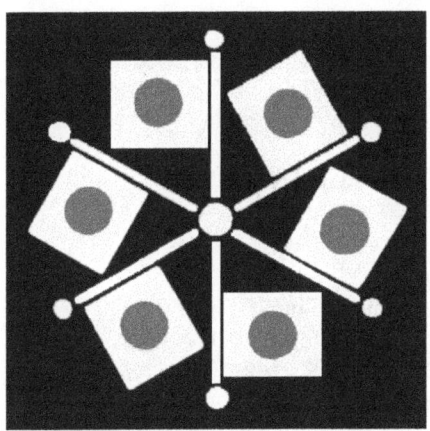

George Ohsawa

George Ohsawa Macrobiotic Foundation
Chico, California

Other books by George Ohsawa in English include: *The Art of Peace; Cancer and the Philosophy of the Far East; Essential Ohsawa; Gandhi, the Eternal Youth; Jack and Mitie; Macrobiotic Guidebook for Living; Macrobiotics: An Invitation to Health and Happiness, Order of the Universe; Philosophy of Oriental Medicine; The Unique Principle; You Are All Sanpaku*; and *Zen Macrobiotics*. Contact the publisher at the address below for a complete list of available titles.

Editing by Kathy Keller
Text layout and design by Carl Ferré
Keyboarding by Alice Salinero

First Edition	1971
Second Printing	1974
Third Printing	1976
Current Edition, edited and reformated	2012 Aug 15

© copyright 1976 by
George Ohsawa Macrobiotic Foundation
  PO Box 3998, Chico, California 95927-3998
  530-566-9765; fax 530-566-9768; *gomf@earthlink.net*
  www.ohsawamacrobiotics.com

Published with the help of East West Center for Macrobiotics
  www.eastwestmacrobiotics.com

ISBN 978-0-918860-06-4

Contents

Introduction — by Herman Aihara	5
Four Hours to Basic Japanese	9
Pronouns	9
Sentence Structure	12
Numbers	13
Prepositions	14
Conjunctions	15
Adjectives	15
Adverbs	16
Verbs	17
Common Expressions	19
Basic Word List	22
Appendix I — Japanese Alphabets and Brain Functions	39
Appendix II — Some Etymology	46
Appendix III — Sentence Patterns	48
Appendix IV — A Japanese Article Written in Roman Alphabet	52
About the Author	54

Introduction
by Herman Aihara

Japanese may be one of the most peculiar languages existing in the world today. The Japanese language is not a member of the Indo-European family, and is neither related to English nor French languages. It is not related to Chinese, even though it has borrowed a large vocabulary from Chinese ideograms. Some Japanese scholars think that Chinese is influenced by Japanese.

George Ohsawa used to say that Japanese is the language of the infinite world. In other words, Japanese has relatively no regulations. It is detached from this world and therefore it can freely express the infinite world. Since it is detached from this world, it often lacks indications of time and space. You can express in any tense simply by using the present tense. However, in the beginning, this lack of time regulation may cause confusion when studying Japanese. This is caused by the fact that you are speaking or writing while thinking in terms of English grammar. In learning Japanese, the most important thing is that you change your concept of the world and its way of expression. To learn Japanese is to learn another way of thinking. Since Japanese was developed by the Japanese mentality, the learning of Japanese entails the assimilation of Japanese thought. From this perspective, studying Japanese is studying Macrobiotics, because the Macrobiotic mentality and principles are the foundation of the Japanese mentality.

The basic differences between Japanese and English are as follows:

1. There are no words corresponding to the articles.

2. There are no plural forms. Therefore, the Japanese word 'tsuma' can mean a wife, wives, the wife, the wives.
3. Japanese rarely use pronouns. They understand the person or thing being talked about through intonations of voice.
4. There is no person or number in verbs.
5. There are no cases for nouns or pronouns. Relations between the words of a sentence are indicated by little words called particles or postpositions (*GA, WA, O, NO, KA*, etc.)
6. There is no infinitive form of verbs.

Contrary to its lack of regulation, Japanese is very particular when indicating courtesy, respect and formality that are often impossible to express in English. These expressions of courtesy, respect, and formality come from the mentality of Japanese who wish to express their deep gratitude, appreciation, and wonder of the orderliness that exists in man as well as in nature.

And finally, the learning of Japanese is the learning of a different art. The Japanese language has created arts called Haiku and Waka, which are simple forms of art. Haiku especially aims at the expression of the order of nature by using only seventeen letters. It seems to me that it is impossible to convey this art in English. It is an art of yin and yang, heaven and earth, flower and bird, mountain and valley. Haiku leads you through ever-changing nature and teaches you an emotionless world. Haiku opens up your mind so that you can see and feel the great nature of the tiny morning dew in the backyard. Japanese expands your mind to infinity.

Of course, it is not an easy job to master such Japanese. This small publication aims at giving you the key to enter the gate leading toward further study of the Japanese language. It is with the utmost pleasure that I am able to serve you with this guide as you once served me with a guide to English or American language.

Introduction 7

Recommended Books for the Study of Japanese:

For those who wish to study Japanese beyond the scope of this introduction, there is a way to continue your study indefinitely beyond the first four hours, even though they are all that is necessary. Those who study Japanese are fortunate to have an excellent series of books known as Naganuma's *Complete Japanese Course*.

1. *Basic Japanese Course*. This is a series of fifty lessons, very short and interesting ones, which take a reader, in the fashion of a children's book, straight through all of the Japanese grammar you will ever need to use—and you will never need to study it again. Japanese grammar is very simple, so simple that Japanese themselves never need to study it in school. It is a clever puzzle—a beautiful mosaic of planned harmony. You will be finished with this course in a few weeks, together with the Grammar and Glossary volume.
2. *Grammar and Glossary*. This volume accompanies the basic course, providing every thing you need to understand it, with all explanations in English.
3. *Standard Japanese Reader, Vol. 1*.
4. *Word Book, Vol. 1*.
5. *Kanji Book, Vol. 1*.

Until this point, all of the writing has been in "Romaji," that is to say, Roman letters, but now you go back over the same lessons quickly in the easy Japanese alphabet, a beautiful one, kana. As you read, the "Chinese characters" are added one by one, in a special order, so that you learn them naturally. The vocabulary is explained in the Word Book, and the characters are completely explained in the Kanji Book.

When you are finished with the lessons you have already learned, you turn the page to begin reading thirty stories, ancient and modern, in many different types and styles of speech, some funny, some beautiful, some practical. All of them explore different aspects of an unknown culture.

There are eight textbooks in all, each with word and kanji books, and additional study materials that are available; only five of them are considered necessary to know almost everything necessary for modern Japanese, while the remaining three lead the student into more ancient forms.

The *Basic Japanese Course* may be obtained from:

The Naganuma Tokyo School of the Japanese Language
38, Nampeidai-Machi
Shibuya-ku, Tokyo Tel.: (463) 7261, 7262

Kyoto Japanese Language School
Ichijo-Dori, Muromachi, Nishi Kamikyo-ku 602
Kyoto Tel.: 431-6737

(The Kyoto School specializes in the "Jordan" modernized text published by Yale University Press.)

Four Hours to Basic Japanese
with the Unique Principle

For English-speaking people, Japanese is probably the easiest major language to learn in spoken form. Four major factors make for this:

1. There is no verb conjugation in basic Japanese, the verb being identical for any person, singular or plural.
2. Simple Japanese can be spoken effectively using the present tense only.
3. Used in this way all verbs are regular and have the same ending: "*masu*."
4. Japanese is the easiest major language to reproduce; all Japanese sounds are easily adapted from English phonetics.

There being no verb conjugation, lengthy memorization of infinitives, multiple endings, etc. is not needed; only one word need be learned for each verb:

I go = *Yukimasu*	We go = *Yukimasu*
You go = *Yukimasu*	You go = *Yukimasu*
He goes = *Yukimasu*	They go = *Yukimasu*
She goes = *Yukimasu*	
It goes = *Yukimasu*	

Pronouns

Singular	Plural
I = *watakushi*	We = *watakusitati*
You = *anata*	You = *anatatati*

He, she = *ano kata*
It = *sore*
This = *kore*
That = *are*

They = *ano katata*
These = *korera*
Those = *arera*

Possessive pronouns are formed by adding the suffix "no."

My = *watakusino*
Our = *watakusitatino*

In conversation, however, a person's name is generally used, rather than the corresponding pronoun.

Several other structural simplifications can streamline learning Japanese:

1. Plural and singular forms of a noun are always identical:

horse = *uma*
horses = *uma*

2. The articles (a, an, and the) do not exist in Japanese.

student = *seito*
a student = *seito*
the student = *seito*
students = *seito*
the students = *seito*

3. Japanese vowels always have the same sound. This pronunciation is roughly the same as Spanish or Italian:

A = the "a" in father (ah)
I = the "i" in machine (ee)
U = the "u" in peruse (oo)
E = the "a" in day (eh)
O = the "o" in go (oh)

The vowels are all spoken very sharply. The most important thing in Japanese pronunciation is to cut the vowel sounds short, never lazily extending them as in English. Once these five vowel sounds are learned, any Japanese word can be spoken with ease.

In the following list, the Japanese phonetic system (the "syllabary edifice") consists of 64 basic syllables, which can be romanized by using the five vowels and fourteen consonants: (parentheses indicate pronunciation)

	A	I	U	E	O
B	ba	bi	bu	be	bo
D	da	di	du	de	do
G	ga	gi	gu	ge	go
H	ha	hi	hu	he	ho
K	ka	ki	ku	ke	ko
M	ma	mi	mu	me	mo
N	na	ni	nu	ne	no
P	pa	pi	pu	pe	po
R	ra	ri	ru	re	ro
S	sa	si (shi)	su	se	so
T	ta	ti (chi)	tu (tsu)	te	to
W	wa	—	—	—	—
Y	ya	—	yu	—	yo
Z	za	zi	zu	ze	zo

The following sounds, introduced from China in the 11th Century, are also used, but much less often:

bya	byu	byo
gya	gyu	gyo
hya	hyu	hyo
kya	kyu	kyo
mya	myu	myo
nya	nyu	nyo
pya	pyu	pyo
rya	ryu	ryo
sya (sha)	syu (su)	syo (sho)
tya (cha)	tyu (chu)	tyo (cho)
zya (ja)	zyu (ju)	zyo (jo)

In various combinations, these 97 sounds form all Japanese words.

Because Japanese is almost wholly unaccented, all syllables receive about the same stress. A particular syllable will thus have the same sound in any word where it occurs. In the examples below, the syllable "*ma*" is pronounced the same in each case. The same holds for any other syllable.

>straight = *massugu*
>stop = *tomaru*
>head = *atama*

There are three syllables that must be given special attention: the *ti*, *si*, and *tu*. The *ti* and *si* incorporate the English "chi" and "shi" sounds. The syllable *ti* = "chi" when spoken; *si* = "shi" when spoken.

>*hati (*pronounced *ha-chi)*
>*watakusi (*pronounced *wa-ta-ku-shi)*

Tu has the sound of "tsu," as in cuts.

>*hitotu (*pronounced *hi-to-tsu)*

This is all the information needed to reproduce Japanese phonetically. Again, the two important things to remember in pronunciation:

1. Any vowel or syllable will always have the same sound whenever used.
2. Vowels are always enunciated very clearly and sharply in contrast to usual spoken English.

Sentence Structure

Japanese syntax is slightly different from that of English. Although adjectives precede nouns in both languages, the Japanese verb is placed at the end of the sentence; the subject is identified by addition of the suffix "*wa*" or "*ga*," and the object is identified by the suffix "*o*."

>English: He eats rice.

Japanese: Anokatawa gohano tabemasu. (He rice eats.)

To ask a question in Japanese, add the word "*ka*" after the verb. To make a negative statement, change the final "*su*" of the verb to "*sen*." To ask a negative question, change the final "*su*" of the verb to "*sen*," and then add the word "*ka*":

> English: He dances.
> *Japanese: Anokatawa odorimasu.*
>
> English: Does he dance?
> *Japanese: Anokatawa odorimasu ka?* (He dances?)
>
> English: He doesn't dance.
> *Japanese: Anokatawa odorimasen.* (He dances not.)
>
> English: Doesn't he dance?
> *Japanese: Anokatawa odorimasen ka?* (He dances not?)

Numbers

Japanese uses two sets of cardinal numbers from one to ten. One set, mainly used by children, is Japanese; the other set is Chinese:

Japanese	*Chinese*
1 = *hitotu*	1 = *iti*
2 = *futatu*	2 = *ni*
3 = *mittu*	3 = *san*
4 = *yottu*	4 = *si*
5 = *itutu*	5 = *go*
6 = *muttu*	6 = *roku*
7 = *nanatu*	7 = *nana*
8 = *yattu*	8 = *hati*
9 = *kokonotu*	9 = *ku*
10 = *to*	10 = *ju*

The numbers after 10 are formed by combining the Chinese numbers with each other and with the Chinese numbers for 100, 1,000, etc. (600 and 800 are the only exceptions):

11 = *ju-iti*	2,000 = *ni-sen*
12 = *ju-ni*	10,000 = *iti-man*
13 = *ju-san*	20,000 = *ni-man*
20 = *ni-ju*	100,000 = *ju-man*
21 = *ni-ju-iti*	200,000 = *ni-ju-man*
30 = *san-ju*	1,000,000 = *hyaku-man*
100 = *hyaku*	10,000,000 = *sen-man*
200 = *ni-hyaku*	100,000,000 = *iti-oku*
600 = *roppyaku,*	1,000,000,000 = *ju-oku*
700 = *hiti-hyaku*	10,000,000,000 = *hyaku-oku*
800 = *happyaku*	100,000,000,000 = *sen-oku*
1,000 = *sen*	1,000,000,000,000 = *iti-tyo*

Notice that in Japanese 10,000 is used as the unit for building higher numbers, as 1,000 is in English; 100,000 is *ju-man* (ten ten-thousands), etc.

Ordinal numbers are formed by adding "*-ban*" to the cardinal numbers:

1st = *iti-ban*
600th = *roppyaku-ban*

Prepositions

(These are approximations as prepositions in any language tend to be used in many idiomatic expressions, and they are often used interchangeably.)

above	*ue*
at	*ni*
by	*de*
for	*tameni*
from	*kara*
in	*ni*
of	*no*
on	*ueni*
to	*e*
under	*sitani*

with (people)	*issyoni*
with (things)	*tō*

Editor's note concerning pronunciation: "*Ju*" (shown on page 11 as the pronunciation of "*zyu*") is the more commonly used written form. "*Mittu*" is pronounced "*mi* (pause)-*tu*" (not "*tsu*" because of the doubled letter). "*Tō*" is pronounced like the English "toe" (a line over a vowel indicates that it is extended — not clipped in the usual way.) "*Ue*" is pronounced like the English "way" but with the vowel clipped, not extended. Other sounds can be figured out by analogy. For the remainder of this series, spellings will be as phonetic as possible. Any word followed by a number will be explained in more detail at the end of this article.

Conjunctions

and = *tō* (plus), *soshite* (then)
but = *keredo*
if = *moshi*
or = *mata*

Adjectives

hot = *atsui*
cold = *samui, tsumetai*
warm = *atatakai*
cool = *suzushi-i*
far = *to-o-i*
near = *chikai*
small = *chi-i-sai*
large = *o-o-ki-i*
glad = *ureshi-i*
sad = *kanashi-i*
skillful = *jo-o-zu-nu, umai*
unskillful = *heta-no*
true = *tadashi-i, makoto-no (1)*
false = *honto-de-nai, uso (2)*
high = *takai*

nervous = *irairashita (3)*
nervous = *ochi/tsukinonai*
right = *migi*
left = *hidari*
full = *ip-pai-no*
empty = *kara-no*
beautiful = *utukushi-i*
ugly = *minikui*
fast = *hayai*
slow = *osoi*
clean = *kirei-nu*
dirty = *kitanai*
wide = *hiroi*
narrow = *semai*
old = *furui*

low = *hikui*
cheap = *yasui*
expensive = *takai*
same = *onaji*
different = *chigau*
salty = *shio-karai*
bitter = *nigai*
sweet = *amai*
sour = *sup-pai*
spicy = *karai*
both = *ryoho*
neither = *doremo*
hard = *katai*
soft = *yawarakai*
calm = *ochitsuita*

new = *atarashi-i*
quiet = *shizuka-nu*
noisy = *urusai*
strong = *tuyoi*
weak = *yowai*
long = *nagai*
short = *mijikai*
easy = *yasashi-i*
difficult = *muzukashi-i*
bad = *warui*
good = *yoi, yoroshi-i (4)*
light = *karui*
heavy = *omoi*
wonderful = *subarashi-i*

Adverbs

again = *mata mo-ichi-do*
always = *itsumo*
before = *saki*

early = *hayaku*
everywhere = *dokodemo*
first = *dai-ichi*
at first = *dai-ichi-ni*
forever = *maeni*
here = *koko-ni*
how = *doshite*
immediately = *sugu-ni*
just = *chodo*
last = *osimai-ni*
late = *osoku*
lately = *chikagoro*
later = *atode*

long ago = *zut-to-mae*
many = *o-o-kuno*
much = *taihen* (also means very)
never = *kes-shite*
now = *ima*
often = *tabi-tabi*
once = *ichi-do*
only = *wazuka-dake*
recently = *saikin*
seldom = *mareni*
sometimes = *toki-doki*
soon = *sugu*
there = *asoko*
when = *itsu*
where = *doko*
why = *naze*

Verbs

accept = *itadaki-masu*
answer = *kotae-masu*
arrive = *tsuki-masu*
ask = *tazune-masu*
be = *ari-masu*
become = *nari-masu*
begin = *hajime-masu*
boil = *ni-masu*
break = *yaburi-masu*
breathe = *iki-shimasu*
breathe = *kokyo-shimasu (5)*
bring = *mot-te ki-masu*
build = *tate-masu*
buy = *kai-masu*
call (aloud) = *yobi-masu*
call (on telephone) = *shimasu*
carry = *mot-te yuki-masu*
catch = *tukami-masu*
change = *kawari-masu*
change = *kae-masu (trans.)*
chant = *kyo-wo-yomi-masu*
close = *shime-masu*
come = *ki-masu*
cross = *watari-masu*
help = *tasuke-masu*
hold = *tamochi-masu*
know (understanding) = *wakari-masu*
know (knowledge) = *shiri-masu*
laugh = *warai-masu*
learn = *narai-masu*
leave (place) = *sari-masu*
leave (thing) = *noko-shimasu*

cry = *naki-masu*
cut = *kid-masu*
dance = *odori-masu*
die = *shini-masu*
do = *shimasu*
drink = *nomi- masu*
dry = *kawaki-masu (6)*
dry = *kawaka-shi-masu (7)*
eat = *tabe-masu*
fall = *ochi-masu*
fight = *tatakai-masu*
fill = *ippai-ni-shimasu*
find = *mitsuke-masu*
finish = *owari-masu*
fix = *naoshi-masu*
forget = *wasure-masu*
get = *e-masu* (many senses, as in English)
give = *age-masu*
go = *yuki-masu*
grow = *seicho-shimasu (6)*
grow = *sodate-masu (7)*
guide = *an-na-i-shimasu*
have = *mochi-masu*
hear = *kiki-masu*
send = *okuri-masu*
show = *mise-masu*
sit = *suwari-masu*
sleep = *ne-masu*
smile = *hohoemi-masu*
speak = *hana-shimasu*
spend = *tsukai-masu*
stand = *tachi-masu*
stand = *todomari-masu (8)*

let = *yuru-shimasu*
life = *age-masu*
like = *suki-masu*
live (be alive) = *ikite-imasu*
look at = *mi -masu*
lose = *ushinai-masu*
love = *ai-shimasu*
make = *tukuri-masu*
meet = *ai-masu*
move = *ugoki-masu*
need = *iri-masu*
open = *hiraki-masu*
play = *asobi-masu*
pull = *hiki-masu*
push = *o-shimasu*
put = *oki-masu*
rain = *furi-masu*
read = *yomi-masu*
receive = *uketori-masu*
remember = *omoida-shimasu*
return = *kaeri-masu (6)*
return = *kae-shimasu (7)*
run = *hashiri-masu*
say = *i-i-masu*
see = *mi-masu*
sell = *uri-masu*

stand = *tomari-masu*
stop = *yame-masu*
stop = *yamesase-masu*
study = *benkyo-shimasu*
sweep = *haki-masu*
swim = *oyogi-masu*
take = *tori-masu*
teach = *oshie-masu*
tell = *hanashi- masu*
thank = *arigato-gozai-masu*
think = *kangae-masu*
touch = *sawari-masu*
try = *tameshi-masu*
understand = *wakari-masu*
use = *tsukai-masu*
visit = *tazune-masu*
wait = *machi-masu*
walk = *aruki-masu*
want = *nozomi-masu*
wash = *arai-masu*
wear = *ki-masu*
welcome = *kangel-shimasu*
win = *kachi-masu*
work = *hataraki-masu*
write = *kaki-masu*

Explanation of Numbered Words: (1) *Tadashi-i* = relatively true, such as 2 + 2 = 4. *Makoto* = absolutely true, such as "Everything changes" or "Yang attracts Yin." (2) *Honto-de-nai* = false. *Uso* = a lie. (3) *Irairashita* = in a trembling state of panic. *Ochitsuki-nonai* = unconfident. (4) *Yoi* = good. *Yoroshi-i* = fine ("I agree"), (5) *Iki-shimasu* is from *i* (life) and *ki* (vital air). *Ko-kyu-shimasu* is from *ko* (exhale) and *kyu* (inhale). (6) Intransitive. (7) Transitive. (8) *Todomari-masu* = to remain. *Tomarimasu* = to stay as a guest.

Common Expressions
(parenthesis are literal translations)

Are you busy?	*Oisogashi-i desu ka?* (Busy is it?)
Be careful.	*Tyui shite kudasai.* (Care do please.)
Come here please.	*Do-ozo kochira e.* (Please here toward.)
Do you like...?	*... o osuki desu ka?*
Do you speak English?	*Eigo o hanashi desu ka?*
Excuse me.	*Gomen nasai.* (Excuse please.)
Good afternoon.	*Kon-nichi-wa.* (This day.)
Good bye.	*Sayonara.*
Good evening.	*Konban-wa.* (This night.)
Good heavens!	*Oya-oya!*
Good luck!	*Gokigen-yo.* (Good feeling I hope.)
Good morning.	*Ohayo.* (Early hello.)
Good night.	*Oyasumi nasai.* (*Oyasumi* = sleep.)
How are you?	*Ogenki desu ka?* (*Genki* = good condition.)
How do you say... in Japanese?	*... wa nihongo de nun to i-i-masu ka?* (*nihogo de nan tō* = Japanese in how)
How many?	*Dorehodo?* (Which amount?)
How much?	*Ikura?*
Hurry up!	*Isoide kudasai!* (Hurry in please.)
I'm going out.	*Dekake-masu.*
I'm hungry.	*Onaka ga suite i-masu.* (Inside empty I am.)
I'm sorry.	*Sumimasen.* (I don't finish. In other words, my sorrow does not end with this apology, which in no way repays you; I am infinitely indebted to you.)
I'm thirsty.	*Nodo ga kawaite i-masu.* (Throat dry is.)
I'm very glad to meet you.	*Oai dekite ureshi-i desu.* (To meet able glad it is.)
I like this.	*Kore ga suki desu.*
I suppose so.	*So-o omoi-masu.*

I think so.	*So-o omoi masu.*
I want to go to bed.	*Mo-o yasumi-masu.* (Now I sleep.)
Is that so?	*So-o desu ka?*
It doesn't matter.	*I-desu.* (Good it is: It's okay either way, I have no preference, etc. This is the mentality—difficult perhaps for a meat-eating Westerner to understand of a person who, in a given situation, though not necessarily all the time, has no preference.)
It's too expensive.	*Takasugi-masu.* (High very it is.)
My name is Sakurazawa Nyoichi.	*watakushi wa Sakurazawa Nyoichi desu.*
Not yet.	*Mada desu.* (Future it is.)
Of course.	*Mochiron desu.* (No discussion it is.)
Please come again.	*Mate irashite kudasai.*
Please help your self.	*Do-ozo agari kudasai.* (*Agari* = step up, come in, make a beginning, etc.)
Quickly!	*Hayaku!*
Quite well, thank you.	*Arigato, genki desu.*
See you again.	*Mata aimasyo.* (*Syo* = future.)
Tell me once more please.	*Mo-o ichi do oshiete kuda-sai.* (*Shiete* = teach.)
Thank you very much.	*Domo arigato.*
Wait a minute please.	*Tyotito mat-te kudasai.* (*Tyot-to* = awhile.)
What can I do for you?	*Nani-ka goyo desu ka?* (What need it is?)
What is that?	*Sore wa nan desu ka?*
What time is it?	*Ima nanji desu ka?* (*Ima* = now.)
Where do you live?	*Doko ni osumai desu ka?* (*Doko ni* = where in.)
Where can I get...?	*...wa doko ni arimasu ka?*
With pleasure.	*Yorokonde.*

You're quite right. *Gomot-tomo dew.*
  (*Mot-tomo* = natural.)
You're very kind. *Anatawa taihen shinsetsu desu.*
You're welcome. *Do-o itashimashite.* (*Do-o*, like *kudasai, o, nasai and go*, is a polite form. *Itashimashite* means I have not done: You're welcome, not at all, etc.)

Colors
red = *aka-iro*
yellow = *ki-iro*
green = *midori-iro*
blue = *ao-iro*
violet = *murasaki-iro*
white = *shiro-iro*
black = *kuro-iro*
black = *hai-iro*
orange = *daidai-iro*
brown = *tya-iro*

Seasons
winter = *huyu*
spring = *ham*
summer = *natsu*
fall = *aki*

Months
January = *ichi-gatsu*
February = *ni-gatsu*
March = *em-gatsu*
April = *shi-gatsu*
May = *go-gatsu*
June = *roku-gatsu*
July = *shichi-gatsu*
August = *hachi-gatsu*

Units of Time
millennium = *sen-nen*
century = *kyaku-nen*
decade = *ju-u-nen*
year = *nen*
month = *tsuki*
week = *syu*
day = *hi*
hour = *ji*
minute = *hun*
second = *byo*

Directions
east = *higashi*
south = *nishi*
west = *minami*
north = *kita*

Days of the Week
Sunday = *nichi yo-o (sun)*
Monday = *getsu yo-o (moon)*
Tuesday = *ka yo-o (fire)*
Wednesday = *sui yo-o (water)*
Thursday = *moku yo-o (wood)*
Friday = *kin yo-o (metal)*
Saturday = *do-yo-o (earth)*

September = *ku-gatsu*
October = *ju-gatsu*
November = *Ju-ichi-gatsu*
December = *ju-ni-gatsu*

Basic Word List
(* indicates English root)

A
ablution = *mizu gori*
abundance = *ho-ofu*
abyss = *ana*
accident = *jiko*
activity = *katsu do*
air = *ku-uki*
albi = *sato imo*
allegiance = *chu setsu*
amusement = *tanoshimi*
anemia = *hin ketsu*
animal = *do-obutsu*
anger = *ikari*

antagonism = *han tai*
antiquity = *mukashi*
anxiety = *shin pai*
appetite = *shokuyoku*
apple = *ringo*
arm = *ude*
army = *rikugun*
art = *geizyutsu*
artist = *geizyutsu-ka*
*atom = *genshi*
awareness = *kizuite iru koto*

B
back = *ushiro*
barley = *o-omugi*
barley tea = *mugi-cha*
basis = *ki so*
bath = *o-huro*
bean = *mame*
beauty = *utukushisa*
*bed = *bed-do*
*beer = *bi-iru*
beginning = *hajime*
bird = *tori*
blood = *ketsueki*
book = *hon*

*boss = *bosu*
bottom = *soko*
bowl = *o-wan*
boy = *shonen*
brain = *no-o*
bread = *pan*
breast = *mune*
breath = *kok yu-u*
brother = *kyo-odd*
brown rice = *gen mai*
buckwheat = *soba*
building = *tatemono*
burdock = *gobo-o*

C

carp = *koi*
carriage = *sha ryo*
carrot = *ninjin*
cat = *neko*
category = *burui*
cause = *gen-in*
caution = *chu-u i*
center man = *nake*
cereal = *koku motsu*
chair = *isu*
change = *ko-okan*
character = *seishitsu*
*cheese = *chi-izu*
chestnut = *kuri*
child = *kodomo*
chlorophyll = *yo-o ryoku so*
cigarette = *tabako*
circle = *maru*
city = *toshi*
clan = *ichi zoku*
clarity = *ak arum*
clothes (Japanese) = *kimono*
clothes (imported) = *yofuku*
cloud = *kumo*

coat = *gaito-o*
command = *mei rei*
communication = *renraku*
community = *bu raku*
companion = *nakama*
completion = *kan sei*
comrade = *sen yu*
concept = *imi*
condition = *jo-oken*
conduct = *ko-o i*
confidence = *ji shin*
conflict = *to-o so-o*
confusion = *kon ran*
constancy = *ken jitsu*
constitution = *tai shitsu*
cooking = *ryori*
corn = *to-omorokoshi*
country = *kuni*
courage = *yu-u-ki*
courtyard = *nakaniwa*
cover = *futa*
cucumber = *kyu-uri*
cure = *chi ryo*

D

dandelion = *tanpopo*
danger = *kiken*
darkness = *kurasa*
date = *hinichi*
daughter = *musume*
day = *hi*
death = *shi*
decay = *otoro-eru-koto*

diet = *shoku-yo-o*
difference = *chigai*
differentiation = *sabetsu-sumkoto*
difficulty = *kon-nan*
*dignity = *ken-i*
dinner = *yu-ushoku*
dining room = *shokudo-o*
direction = *ho-oko-o*

decision = *ket-tei*
decrease = *heru koto*
deed = *ko-oi*
defeat = *makeru-koto*
defense = *bo-ogyo*
democracy = *minshushugi*
dentist = *haisha*
departure = *shuppa-tsu*
dependence = *tayoru-koto*
desert = *sabaku*
desire = *yoku-bo-o*
desk = *tsukue*
dessert = *deza-ato*
detachment = *cho-zen*
detail = *sho-osai*
development = *hat-ta-tsu*
devil = *ah-ma*
devotion = *ken-shin*
diabetes = *to-onyo-obyo-o*
diarrhea = *ge-ri*
diary = *nik-ki*

discipline = *shu-gyo-o*
discovery = *hak-ken*
discussion = *boron*
disease = *byo-o-ki*
disgrace = *chi-joku*
dish = *o-sara*
disorder = *mu-chitsu-jo*
dispersion = *kai-san*
distance = *kyo-ri*
distinction = *sa-betsu*
doctor = *isha*
dog = *inu*
door = *to*
doubt = *utagai*
dough = *pan-dane*
dragon = *ryu*
dream = *yume*
drug = *yakuhin*
drum = *tai-ko*
duration = *kei-zoku-ki-kan*
duty = *gimu*

# E
ear = *mimi*
earth = *chikyu*
economy = *keizai*
edge = *hashi*
education = *kyo-oiku*
egg = *tamago*
electricity = *denki*
element = *yo-oso*
embassy = *taishikan*
end = *owari*
enemy = *teki*
enthusiasm = *nes-shin*

environment = *kankyo-o*
epilepsy = *tenkan*
error = *aya-mari*
esteem = *son-cho-o*
evil = *aku-ma*
example = *rei*
exception = *reigai*
excess = *yobun*
exercise = *undo-o*
exhaustion = *tsukare-hateru-koto*
expansion = *bo-ocho-o*
experience = *keiken*

entrance = *iriguchi*
envelope = *hu-uto-o*

F
face = *kao*
fact = *jijitsu*
factor = *yo-oso*
factory = *ko-oba*
fad = *hayari*
faith = *shinrai*
fame = *mei-yo*
family = *kazoku*
farm = *no-ojo-o*
fanner = *no-oka*
fast = *danjiki*
fat = *shi-bo-o*
fate (destiny) = *unmei*
father = *otosan*
fatigue = *tsukare*
fault = *ayama-chi*
fear = *osore*
focus = *sho-oten*
follower = *shitagafu-mono*
following = *tsui zui*
folly = *orokasa*
food = *shoku-motsu*
fool = *bakana-hito*
foot = *kata-ashi*
foreigner = *gaijin*
*fork = *ho-oku*
form = *katachi*

G
gall bladder = *tan-no-o*
game (play) = *shobu-goto*

expert = *jukuren shitahito*
eye = *me*

feces = *dai ben*
fee = *ryo-okin*
fellowship = *naka-ma*
female = *josei*
fence = *saku*
fever = *netsu-byo-o*
field = *nohara*
fight = *tatakai*
finger = *yubi*
fire = *hi*
fish = *sakana*
flame = *honoho*
flexibility = *ju-unan-sa*
flood = *ko-ozui*
floor = *yuka*
flour = *komugiko*
flower = *hana*
fly = *hae*
fortune (wealth) = *zaisan*
foundation = *kiso*
fowl = *ahiru*
freedom = *jiyu-u*
friend = *tomo, yu-ujin*
front = *mae*
frontier = *kok-kyochiho-o*
fruit = *kudamono*
fun = *omoshi-roi-koto*
future = *mirai*

goose = *gacho-o*
government = *seihu*

game (animal) = *emono*
garden = *niwa*
gate = *mon*
generosity = *kandai*
gentlemen = *shinshi*
gift = *okuri-mono*
ginger = *sho-oga*
girl = *sho-ojo*
gland = *sen*
glasses = *megane*
gluttony = *tai-shoku*
goal = *moku-hyo-o*
goat = *yagi*
god = *kami*
gold = *kin*
good = *yoikoto*

grace = *shitoyakasa*
grain = *kokumotsu*
grandmother = *o-ba-asan*
grandfather = *o-ji-isan*
grass = *kusa*
gratitude = *kan-sha*
greatness = *idaina-koto*
grocery = *yawoya*
ground = *jimen*
group = *atsumari*
growth = *seicho-o*
guest = *o-kyaku*
guidance = *michibiki*
guilt = *shizukesa*
*gun = *gan*

H
habit = *shu-ukan*
hair = *kaminoke*
halibut = *hirame*
hammer = *kanazuchi*
hand = *katate*
happiness = *ko-ohuku*
harbor = *minato*
harmony = *cho-owa*
hat = *bo-oshi*
hatred = *nikushimi*
hawk = *taka*
head = *atama*
headache = *zutsu-u*
health = *kenko-o*
heart = *shin-zo-o*
heaven = *ten-goku*
heat = *netsu*

hill = *oka*
hindrance = *kon-nan*
Hinduism = *Indo-kyo-o*
hint = *anji*
history = *rekishi*
hole = *ana*
holiday = *yasumi*
home = *katei*
honesty = *sho-ojiki*
honey = *hachimitsu*
hope = *kibo-o*
horse = *uma*
hospital = *byo-oin*
host = *aruji*
hostess = *onna aruji*
hour = *jikan*
house = *ie*

hell = *jigoku*
help = *enjo*
helper = *tetsudai*
hemoglobin = *kek-kyu*
hen = *mendori*
herb = *yakuso-o*
hesitation = *chu-cho*

humanity = *jinrui*
humiliation = *kutsu-joku*
humility = *ken-son*
humor = *ton-chi*
husband = *ot-to*
hut = *koya*

I
ice = *ko-ori*
*ice cream = *aisuku-ri-imu*
idea = *kangae*
ideal = *riso-o*
ignorance = *muchi*
imagination = *so-ozo-o*
importance = *ju-uyo-osei*
impression = *insho-o*
improvement = *kai-ryo-o*
impulse = *shi-geki*
increase = *zo-oka*
independence = *dokuritsu*
individual = *ko-jin*
individuality = *ko-sei*
infinity = *mu-gen*
inflammation = *nen-sho-o*

influence = *ei-kyo-o*
information = *jo-oho-o*
inn = *yado-ya*
innocence = *mu-zai*
insanity = *kichigai*
insect = *kontyu-u*
inside = *nai-bu*
insomnia = *humin-sho-o*
inspiration = *reikan*
instinct = *hon-no-o*
interest = *kyo-omi*
interruption = *samatage*
intestines = *cho-o*
intuition = *choku-kan*
invention = *hatsumei*
island = *shima*

J
Japan = *Nihon, Nippon*
jewel = *ho-oseki*
job = *shigoto*
joy = *yorokobi*
judge = *saibankan*
judgment = *handan*
justice = *seigi*

K
key = *kagi*
kidney = *zin-zo-o*
kindness = *shinsetsu*
king = *wo-osama*
kingdom = *wo-okoku*
kitchen = *daidokoro*
knife = *ko-gatana*
knowledge = *chi-shiki*

L

lake = *mizu-umi*
land = *rikuchi*
language = *kotoba*
laundry = *sentakuya*
law (natural) = *ho-osoku*
law (man made) = *ho-oritsu*
laziness = *nama-keru-koto*
leader = *shido-osha*
leaf = *hap-pa*
leap = *hiyaku*
leg = *ashi*
lesson = *jugyo-o*
letter = *tegami*
liar = *usotsuki*
library = *toshokan*

lie = *uso*
life = *jin-sei*
light = *hikari*
lightening = *kaminari*
limit = *gendo*
limitation = *genkai*
lip = *kuchibiru*
liquid = *ekitai*
liver = *kanzo-o*
logic = *ron-ri*
loss = *son-shitsu*
lotus = *hasu*
love = *ai*
loyalty = *chu-gi*
lunch = *chu-shoku*
lung = *hai*

M

Macrobiotics = *shoku-yo-o*
magazine = *zas-shi*
magnet = *jishaku*
mail = *yu-ubin*
man = *hito*
manager = *shihai-nin*
mankind = *jin-rui*
manner = *taido*
map = *chizu*
mare = *roba*
market = *shijo-o*
marriage = *kek-kon*
massage = *momi-ryo-oji*
master = *shujin*
mathematics = *su-ugaku*
matter = *bus-shitsu*

merchant = *sho-o-nin*
message = *koto-zuke*
metal = *kinzoku*
method = *ho-oho-o*
middle = *man-naka*
milk = *gyu-unyu-u*
mind = *kokoro*
minister (gov't) = *daijin*
minister (serve) = *tsukaeru*
miracle = *kiseki*
mirror = *kagami*
misery = *higeki*
misfortune = *fu-un*
mission = *shimei*
mistake = *ayamachi*
modesty = *shis-so*
moment = *shun-kan*

meadow = *boku-jo-o*
meaning = *imi*
meat = *niku*
mechanism = *ki-ko-o*
medicine = *kusuri*
meditation = *mei-so-o*
meeting = *kaigo-o*
melon = *uri*
memory = *kioku*
meningitis = *no-o-maku-en*
menstruation = *gek-kei*
mentality (mental condition) = *sei-shin jo-otai*

money = *o-kane*
monkey = *saru*
moon = *tsuki*
morality = *do-otoku*
mother = *oka-asan*
motion = *ugoki*
mountain = *yama*
mouth = *kuchi*
movement = *undo-o*
movie = *eiga*
murder = *satsujin*
music (sound-study) = *on-gaku*

N

name = *namae*
nation = *kokka*
nature (character) = *seishitsu*
nature = *shizen*
necessity = *hitsuyo*
neck = *kubi*
needle = *had*
neighbor = *rinjin*
nephew = *oi*
nerve = *shinkei*
nervous system = *shinkei-keito*
nest = *su*
news = *shirase*

niece = *mei*
night = *yoru*
nightmare = *akumu*
noise = *so-on*
noodles = *udon*
noon = *ma-hiru*
nose = *hana*
nourishment = *eiyo-o*
number = *kazu*
nut = *ki-no-mi*

O

oats = *kashi*
obesity = *himan*
object = *mokuteiki*
objection = *igi*
observation = *kansatsu*

onion = *tamanegi*
opera = *kageki*
operation = *so-osa*
opinion = *iken*
opposite = *hansuru-mono*

obstruction = *jama*
offering = *sonae-mono*
office = *jimusho*
oil = *abura*
omelet = *tamago-yaki*
oneself (self body) = *jishin*
oneself (differentiation) = *ware*
   (Big Self = *Tai-Ga*)
   (ego = *ga*)

P
pace = *ayumi*
package = *tsutsumi*
pain = *itami*
paint = *toryo-o*
pan = *nabe*
pancreas = *sui-zo-o*
paper = *kami*
paralysis = *mahi*
paranoia (off-balance, rigid
   mentality) = *henshukyo*
parasite = *kiseichu-u*
parent = *ryo-oshin*
park = *ko-oen*
part = *bubun*
partner = *kyo-odo-o-sha*
party = *enkai*
passenger = *jo-okyaku*
passion = *jo-onetsu*
past = *kako*
path = *michi*
peace = *heiwa*
peach = *momo*
peak = *cho-oten*
peanut = *nankinmame*

opposition = *hantai*
oppression = *appaku*
order (-liness) = *chitsujo*
organ (body) = *kikan*
originality = *dokuso-osei*
outside = *gaibu*
oven = *kamado*
overcoat = *gaito-o*
ox = *ushi*
oyster = *kaki*

pleasure = *tanoshimi*
plum = *sumomo*
poem = *shi*
poet = *shijin*
point (geometric) = *ten*
poison = *doku*
pole (axis) = *kyoku*
pole (post) = *sao*
police = *junsa*
police station = *ko-oban*
politeness = *reigitadashisa*
pool = *oyogiba mizutamari*
population = *jinko-o*
postage stamp = *kitte*
post card = *hagaki*
post office = *yubin-kyoku*
pot = *tsubo*
potassium = *karyum*
*potato = *poteito*
powder = *kona*
power = *tikara*
practice = *renshu-u*
praise = *sho-osan*
prayer = *inori*

pearl = *shinju*
peasant = *hiakusho-o*
*pen = *pen*
penalty = *batsu*
pencil = *enpitsu (lead brush)*
penis = *yinkei*
people = *hitobito*
permission = *kyoka*
perseverance = *nintai*
person = *kojin*
perversion = *kyoku-kai*
pet = *higan-do-obutsu*
pheasant = *kiji*
philosopher = *tetsugakusha*
philosophy = *tetsugaku*
photography = *shashin jutsu*
photograph = *shashin*
physics = *butsuri*
piece = *kakera*
pig = *buta*
pigeon = *hato*
pineal gland = *sho-oka tai*
place = *basho*
plan = *keikaku*
plant = *shokubutsu*
plaster (compress) = *ko-oyaku*
plate = *o-sara*
play (game) = *asobi*
play (theatre) = *geki*

preparation = *junbi*
present (gift) = *okurimono*
present (tense) = *genzai*
pressure = *atsuryoku*
price = *nedan*
pride = *hokori*
priest = *bokushi*
prince = *wo-oji*
princess = *wo-oji*
principle = *gensoku*
prison = *ro-ogoku*
problem = *mondai*
process = *katei*
product = *seihin*
professor = *kyo-oju*
profit = *rieki*
progress = *shinpo*
promise = *yakusoku*
protest = *shucho*
prune = *kanso-o-shita-sumomo*
psychology = *shinrigaku*
public hall = *ko-okaido-o*
pulse = *myakuhaku*
*pump = *ponpu*
pumpkin = *kabocha*
punishment = *batsu*
purchase = *kai-ire*
purpose = *mokuteki*
purse = *saihu*

# Q
quality = *shitsu*
quantity = *ryo-o*

question = *shitsumon*

R

race (people) = *jinshu*
race (contest) = *kyoso-o*
rain = *ame*
rank = *kaikyu-u*
rat = *nezumi*
ray = *ho-oshasen*
reaction = *han-no-o*
reason = *nyu-u*
rebirth = *umarekawari*
reception = *uketsuke*
recipe = *ryori-no-shikata*
reduction = *shukusho-o*
reference = *sanko-o*
regimen = *rentai*
regret = *ko-okai*
relationship = *kankei*
religion = *shu-ukyo-o*
remorse = *kuiru-koto*
repair = *shu-uri*
report = *ho-okoku*
repulsion = *hanpatsu*
request = *yo-o* = *kyu-u*
resentment = *urami*
residence = *kyoju-u*
resistance = *teiko-o*
resoluteness = *kaiketsu*
respect = *soncho-o*
responsibility = *sekinin*
rest = *kyu-usoku*
result = *kekka*
retreat = *ko-otai*
return = *kaeru-koto*
revolution = *kakumei*
reward = *ho-oshu-u*
rhythm = *choshi*
rice = *kome*
rigidity = *ganko-nakoto*
ring = *wa*
river = *kawa*
road = *do-oro*
rock = *iwa*
roof = *yane*
room = *heya*
root = *ne*
rope = *tsuna*
rose = *bara*
rule = *kisoku*
rye = *karasu-mugi*

S

sack = *hukuro*
sacrifice = *gisei*
*salad = *sarada*
salad (pressed) = *tsukemono*
salary = *kyu-uryo*
saliva = *tsuba*
salmon = *sake*
severity = *kibishi-sa*
sex = *sei*
shadow = *kage*
shame = *haji*
shape = *katachi*
sheep = *hitsuji*
shell = *kaigara*

salt = *shio*
sand = *suna*
sanity (health mind) =
   kenzen-no-kokoro
satisfaction = *manzoku*
*sauce = *so-osu*
schizophrenia (separation
   symptom) = *bunretsu-sho-o*
scallion = *negi*
scale = *hakari*
school = *gakko*
science = *kagaku*
screw = *neji*
sea = *umi*
search = *tan kyu-u*
season = *kisetsu*
seat = *zaseki*
seaweed = *kaiso-o*
secret = *himitsu*
secretary = *hisho*
section = *kubun*
seed = *tane*
sense = *kankaku*
sentence (words) = *bun*
sentence (punishment) =
   hanketsu
sentiment = *shin-jo-o*
sentimentality = *kan-sho-o*
separation = *bunri*
series = *renzoku*
service = *ho-oshi*
sesame oil = *goma-abura*
sesame paste = *neri-goma*
sesame salt = *goma-shio*
sesame seed = *goma*

ship = *hune*
shock = *sho-ogeki*
shoe = *kutsu*
shop = *mise*
shoulder = *kata*
shout = *sakebi*
shower = *niwaka-ame*
sickness = *byo-oki*
side = *sokumen*
sieve = *furui*
sight = *shiryoku*
sign = *shirushi*
silence = *chinmoku*
silk = *kinu*
silver = *gin*
simplicity = *kanso*
sincerity = *seijitsu*
sister = *onna-kyo-odai*
situation = *jo-otai*
skin = *hada*
sky = *sora*
slave = *dorei*
slavery = *dorei-seido*
sleep = *suimin*
sleeve = *sode*
slice = *kirimi*
slipper = *uwabaki*
slope = *saka*
smell = *nioi*
smile = *emi*
smoke = *kemuri*
snake = *hebi*
snow = *yuki*
society = *shakai*
socket = *sashikomi*

sodium = *natoryumu*
soil = *tsuchi*
solar plexus = *taiyo-o-shinkei-so-o*
soldier = *gunjin*
sole = *ashi-no-ura*
solution (to a problem) = *kaiketsu*
son = *musuko*
song = *uta*
sorrow = *kanashimi*
soul = *tamashi-i, reikon*
sound = *oto, on*
soup = *shiru*
source = *minamoto*
soy bean = *daizu*
soy paste = *miso*
soy sauce, tamari = *sho-oyu*
space = *ku-ukan*
spark = *hibana*
specialization = *tokushu-ka*
specialty = *tokushoku*
speech = *enzetsu*
speed = *sokudo*
spice = *yakumi*
spinach = *ho-orenso-o*
spiral = *rasen*
spirit = *seishin*
spleen = *hizo-o*
spoon = *saji*
sport = *undo-kyogi*
spot (location) = *basho*
squash (pumpkin) = *kabocha*
stair = *hashigo*
stamina = *tairyoku*

station = *eki*
steam = *jo-oki*
steel = *hagane*
step = *ippo*
stimulation = *shigeki*
stomach = *i*
stone = *ishi*
store = *sho-oten*
story (tale) = *monogatari*
stove = *kamado*
strainer = *kosu-mono*
straw = *wara*
strawberry = *ichigo*
stream = *nagare*
street = *to-ori*
strength = *tsuyosa*
strike = *dageki*
string = *himo*
struggle = *to-oso-o*
study = *benkyo-o*
style = *katachi*
sublimity = *su-uko-o*
substance = *naiyo-o*
subway = *chikatetsu*
success = *seiko-o*
sugar = *sato-o*
suicide = *zisatsu*
sun = *taiyo*
supply = *kyo-okyu-u*
support = *sasae*
surprise = *odoroki*
surrender = *ko-ofuku*
sweat = *ase*
swelling = *mukumi*
symbol = *sho-ocho-o*

standard = *hyo-ojun*
star = *hoshi*
state (condition) = *jo-otai*
system = *soshiki*

T
table = *tsukue*
Taoism = *Do-o-kyo-o*
taro (albi) = *sato-imo*
tea = *(o-) cha*
teacher = *sensei*
teaching = *oshie*
tea pot = *dobin*
tear (cry) = *nakukoto*
technique = *gijitsu*
temple = *tera*
therapy = *chiryo-o*
thing = *monokoto*
thinking = *kangaeru-koto*
thoroughness = *kangae-bukai*
thought = *kangae*
thrift = *shisso*

U
understanding = *rikai*
unhappiness = *fuko-o*
unification = *to-oitsu*
union = *ittai*
universe = *uchu-u*

W
war = *senso-o*

sympathy = *dojo-o*
symphony (entwined echo pleasure) = *ko-o kyo-o gaku*
synthesis = *go-osei*

thumb = *oyayubi*
thunder = *kaminari*
time = *jikan*
toast = *kanpai*
tongue = *shita*
tooth = *ha*
toothache = *haitami*
town = *machi*
transmutation = *tenkan*
treasure = *zaisan*
treatment = *chiryo-o*
tree = *ki*
trout = *masu*
truth = *shinri*
tuberculosis = *haibyo*

V
vagina = *chitsu*
value = *neuchi*
variety = *tashu-tayo-o*
vegetable = *yasai*
vessel = *iremono*
vibration = *shindo-o*
violence = *bo-oryoku*
virtue = *toku*

will = *ishi*

waste = *muda*
water = *mizu*
watercress = *mizuta-garashi*
waterfall = *taki*
watermelon = *suika*
way = *michi, ho-o-ho-o*
weakness = *yowasa*
wealth = *tomi*
weapon = *buki*
well = *ido*
wheat = *komugi*
wife = *tsuma*

wind = *kaze*
window = *mado*
wine = *(o-) sake*
wisdom = *chie*
woman = *onna-no-hito, jo-sei*
wood = *mokuzai*
work = *shigoto*
world = *sekai*
worry = *shinpaigoto*
wound = *kizu*
writer = *sho-osetsuka*

Y

Yang = *Yo-o*
yang = *yo-o-sei* [see page 37 for a discussion of *yo-o-sei* and *(y)in-sei*]
year = *toshi*
yeast = *ko-oji*
Yin = *(Y)in* (the "Y" is not pronounced)
yin = *(y)in-sei* (the "y" is not pronounced)
youth = *seinen*

Z

zeal = *netchu-u*
zoology = *dobutsu-gaku*

Addenda
abdomen = *hukubu*
agriculture = *no-ogyo-o*
appendix = *mo-ocho-o*
arrogance = *go-oman*
baby = *akanbo*
biology = *seibutsu-gatu*
bladder = *bo-oko-o*

church = *kyo-okai*
circulation = *junkan*
*coffee = *ko-ohi-i*
company = *haisha*
concentration = *shu-u-chu-u*
connection = *kankei*
consciousness = *ishiki*

blindness = *mo-omoku*
bridge = *hashi*
Buddhism = *Bukkyo-o*
cancer = *gan*
chicken = *niwa-tori*
chemistry = *ka-gaku*
chopsticks = *hashi*
*Christianity = *Kiristo-kyo-o*

constipation = *benpi*
contraction = *shu-ushuku*
control = *tosei*
cook = *ryo-ori*
cow = *ushi*
creation = *so-ozo-o*
criticism = *hihan*
cup = *(o)-wan*
custom = *shu-u-kan*

(Ed: A brief review of Japanese pronunciation):

1. *Each syllable is pronounced distinctly, without accent.*
2. *Vowel pronunciation is roughly equivalent to Spanish:*

    A = the a in 'car' (ah)
    E = the e in 'end' (eh)
    I = the i in 'machine' (ee)
    O = the o in 'go' (oh)
    U = the u in 'rule' (oo)

3. *Japanese vowels should be cut very short and enunciated very clearly. The only exceptions will be indicated here by doubling the vowel, with a hyphen between, which indicates that the vowel sound should be held about twice as long as usual. It does not mean that the vowel sound should be pronounced twice. For example, YIN and YANG, (Y)in and Yo-o, (y)in-sei and yo-o-sei.*

During different dynastic periods in China, various words had more than one pronunciation, "yin" and "yang" being examples. At one time, they were pronounced *(Y)in (een)* and *Yo-o*. In Japan, *(Y)in* and *Yo-o* are used. (Since the "Y" in "Yin" is not pronounced in Japan, it shouldn't be there, but the custom has been to leave it.)

Lao Tzu said:

"*Nature first begets one thing. Then one thing begets another. The two produce a third. In this way, all things*

are begotten. Why?? Because all things are impregnated by two alternating tendencies... which, acting together, complement each other."
(Tao Teh King, A.J. Baum translation)

These "two alternating tendencies" are Yin and Yang, which create and destroy all phenomena. In the Far East, after centuries of objective and systematic observation, this understanding became the basis of the way of life, the principle upon which one relied as the basis of logic and action: Yin and Yang, the way of Nature, the law of Change, the Unique or Unifying Principle, polarizable monism, the principle of complementary antagonism.

(Y)in-sei and *Yo-o-sei*, on the other hand, mean *that which is in a yin* (expansive, watery, cold, feminine, passive, vegetal, etc.) *state*, and *that which is in a yo-o* (contractive, dry, hot, masculine, active, animal, etc.) *state*. In other words, to say "He is yin" is not really accurate; it means he is absolutely and forever yin, Yin itself, but one is really only *presently manifesting* Yin or Yang (actually both, of course). So it would be more accurate to say "He is *yin-sei*." (*Sei* means character, quality, state, condition, nature, etc.) Everything is *made by* Yin and Yang, never *equal to* Yin or Yang. (Or both: as part of the whole, we can never equal it.)

Appendices by Herman Aihara

Appendix 1

Japanese Alphabets and Brain Functions

Japanese believe that everything expresses itself by voice — even lifeless things such as rivers, trees, and mountains. However, man is far superior in voice-communication compared with other animals, plants, or things. Pavlov called words the second communication system because he thought that shape and color are the first communication system. The second system requires a higher function of the brain than the first system. Therefore, it can be disturbed easily in case of fatigue or sleepy conditions. When one is sleepy, the second system stops functioning but not the first system.

How do words express our thoughts, feelings, and emotions? Electrical and chemical changes in the brain produce thoughts, feelings, and emotions that in turn cause the activation of the motor nerves. This activated nerve system causes the action of the mouth muscles. Words are produced with the coordination of mouth muscles as they move and as air is exhaled. Physiologically, the voice is controlled by the cerebral cortex and corpus callosum in the brain. When words are heard, the same pattern of stimulation occurs in the corresponding area of the brain. Through this pattern of activation in the brain, we can reproduce thoughts, feelings, and emotions similar to those that were created in another's brain. In this way, words or voices are able to convey thoughts, feelings, and emotions.

All words are made of vowels and consonants. However, the main parts of any word are vowels. When you produce vowels, you exhale from the abdomen but when you produce consonants, you exhale from the mouth. Consonants are sounds produced merely by mouth movement but vowels are produced by the whole body. Therefore, in any language, vowels are the foundation of words. Roughly speaking, any language consists of five vowels, "AEIOU." (Here, "A" is "ah" sound.)

In order to produce these sounds, a specific area of the brain must be activated. Specifically, "A" as a sound is the result of the frontal lobe function; the "E" sound is the result of the parietal lobe function; "I" is the result of the central lobe function; "O" is the result of the temporal lobe and cerebellum functions; and finally, "U" is the result of the corpus callosum and brain stem function. (See diagram on page 41.)

In other words, whenever the sound of "A" is produced, the frontal lobe has been stimulated. Even when the sound of "A" is heard, the frontal lobe is stimulated. Furthermore, each vowel stimulates its corresponding area of the brain, which produces the particular thoughts, feelings, and emotions.

For example, the frontal lobe reveals the highest function of brain capacities such as abstraction, aspiration, imagination, wonderful feelings, and gratitude. The parietal lobe reveals, or is associated with, recognition, intellect, and discrimination. The central lobe is associated with sense perception. The temporal lobe and cerebellum are associated with emotion, volition, and action. The corpus callosum plus the interbrain and the brain stem are associated with mechanical, intuitive, and autonomic activities.

Therefore, the judgment of abstraction, aspiration, imagination, wonderful feelings, and gratitude is improved or stimulated by the "A" sound or voicing the "A" sound. In Sanskrit, "A" is an original life force. In the Shingon Sect of Buddhism, Aji (Word) Meditation concentrates on the words A and the meaning of A. In English, an article "a" means wonderful and aspiration. The English article "a" must start with wonderfulness when someone finds a bread on the table when he was hungry. So he says, "Oh! A bread!" instead of saying, "Oh! The bread!" Because "the" has the sound of "I," this corresponds to sense. In other words, "the bread" means that the

Japanese Alphabets and Brain Functions

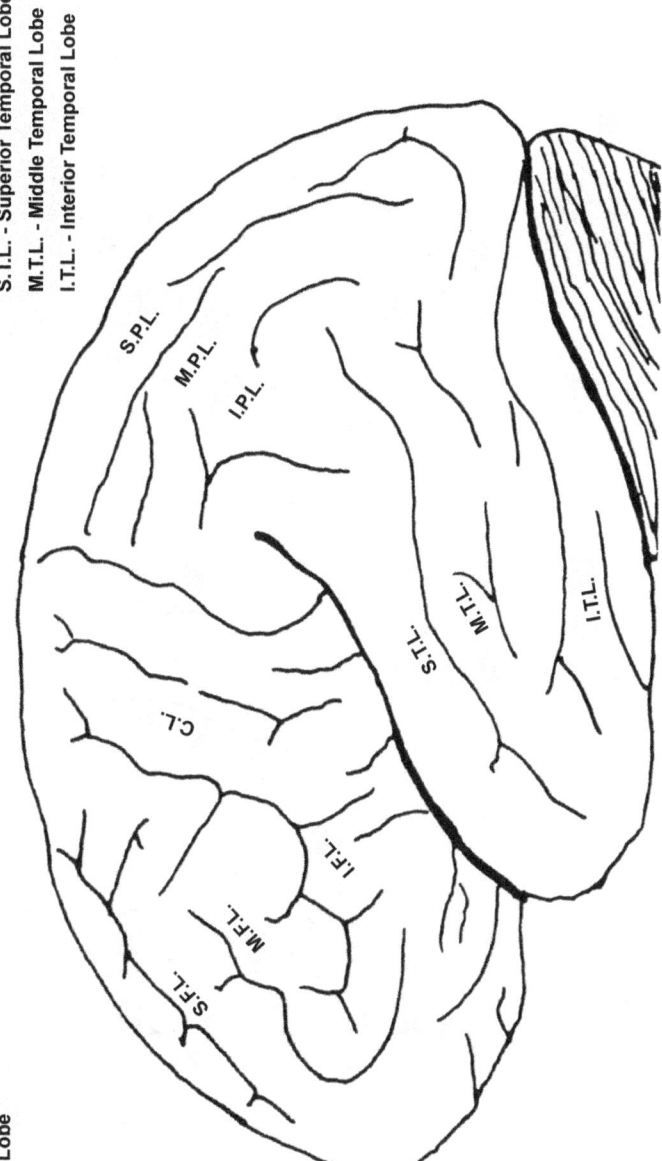

Lateral Aspect of the Brain

S.F.L. - Superior Frontal Lobe
M.F.L. - Middle Frontal Lobe
I.F.L. - Interior Frontal Lobe
C.L. - Central Lobe

S.P.L. - Superior Parietal Lobe
M.P.L. - Middle Parietal Lobe
I.P.L. - Interior Parietal Lobe
S.T.L. - Superior Temporal Lobe
M.T.L. - Middle Temporal Lobe
I.T.L. - Interior Temporal Lobe

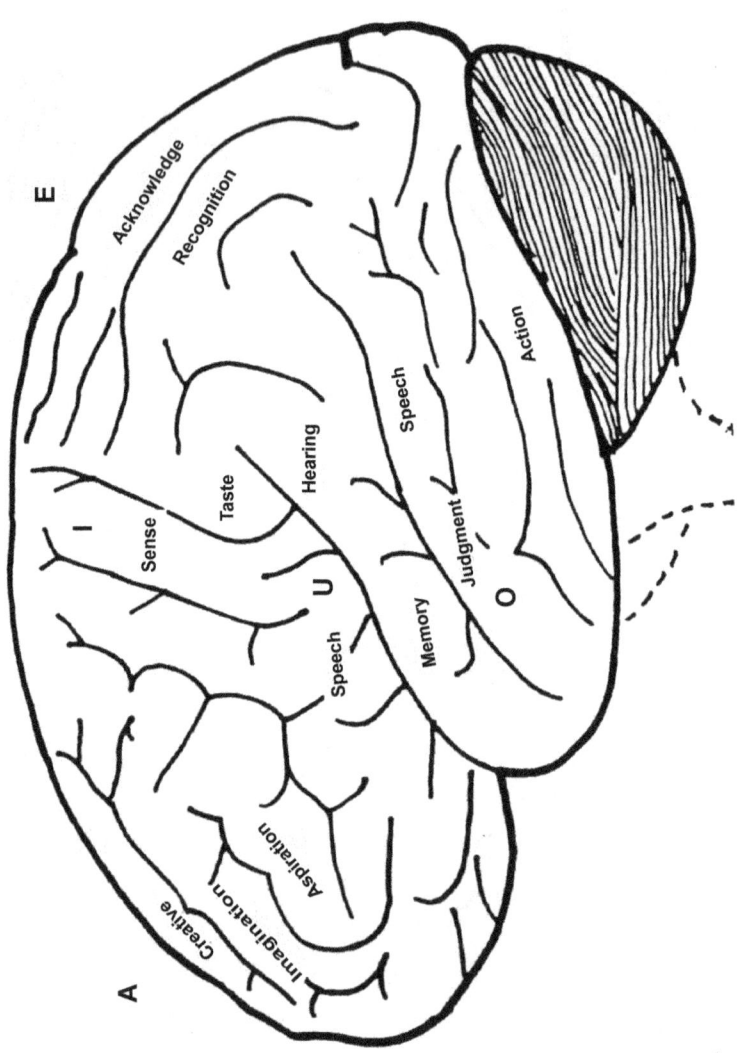

bread has a certain smell, color, and shape so that it is distinguished from other breads. Therefore, sensory perception is improved by voicing "I." (See diagram on page 42.)

The "E" sound relates to recognition, intellect, and memory as used in words such as memory, education, knowledge, etc. Therefore, the judgment of intellect, recognition, and memory is improved by the voicing of "E." The "O" sound relates to emotion, volition, and action as expressed in words such as War, Go, Do. Therefore, the action is strengthened by voicing the "O" sound. The "U" sound relates to intuition and autonomic activities. Animals snarl before they jump on their prey. When we have pain, we will say "uuuuuuuu" holding the painful part. The intuitive and autonomic activities are improved by the voicing of "U."

The influence of vowel sounds on brain functions is comparable to psychological theories.

Pavlov	**Freud**	**Brain Area**	**Dr. Magoun**	**Sound**
		frontal lobe	gratitude, wonderfulness	A
second signal system	super ego	parietal lobe	recognition intellect memory	E
first signal system	super ego	central lobe	sense perception	I
conditioned reflex	ego	temporal lobe	emotion volition learned action	O
unconditional reflex	ID	thalamus hypothalamus	protective action metabolic action	U

Lateral Aspect of the Brain

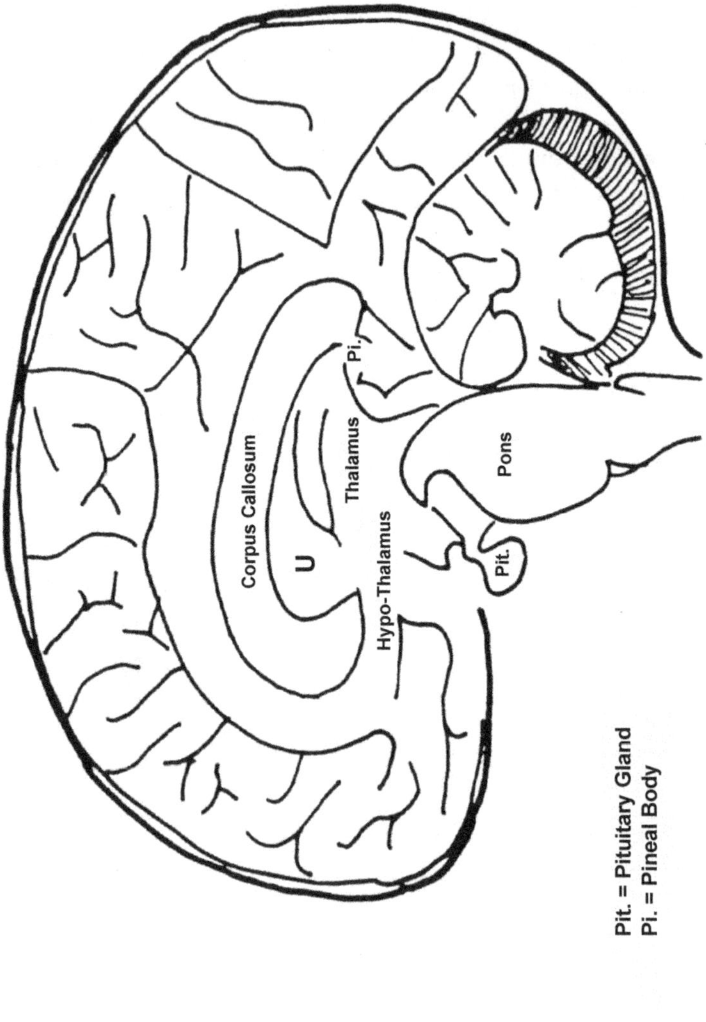

Corpus Callosum
Thalamus
Pi.
Hypo-Thalamus
Pons
Pit.

Pit. = Pituitary Gland
Pi. = Pineal Body

Summary of Vowels:

A sound (produced with the mouth wide open): We make this sound when we are surprised or admiring.

E sound: We produce this sound when we are inquiring.

I sound: This sound is made when we describe things by using adjectives such as pretty, pitiful, etc. Japanese adjectives almost always finish with "i."

O sound: O is an action sound. Animals attack their prey with the sound of OO.

U sound: This sound is a sound of life. When you have pain, you will say oo. Japanese verbs almost always finish with "u." The regular stem is "u," and the regular conversational form is "masu."

The Indian and Chinese languages contain many A and U sounds. Therefore, they are less sensorial and contain less conceptuality; they are more intuitive than the Western languages that contain much E sound, which makes Westerners more analytical and conceptually intelligent. Japanese language contains many I sound. Therefore, Japanese language is soft and sensitive and delicate. It is very beneficial for Easterners to learn the Western languages and for Westerners to learn the Eastern languages.

Appendix 2

Some Etymology

Many words now used in Japanese are of Chinese origin and not pure Japanese. Here I will show you some of the etymology of pure Japanese, which is still in use.

1. *Haru* — Spring (season). The original meaning of this word is to pull a bow fully and also "full of potentiality." In spring, the soil reserves the growing power fully so that all seeds spring up. Such a condition is *Haru*.

2. *Aki* — Fall (season). *Aki* means originally space, or emptiness. In autumn, leaves fall down and branches become bare so that spaces between branches increase. Therefore, autumn is called *aki* (bare trees).

Aki-ma — empty room or room for rent. (This is Chinese origin. *Ma* is a room.)

Aki-ya — an empty house or renting house. (This is also Chinese origin. *Ya* means house.)

3. *Aka* — red color. Probably this word came from *Aki* when leaves redden.

4. *Ki* — This means yellow color and also life energy. Grains and vegetables (most of them) ripen in autumn and become yellow and full of energy (*ki*).

5. *Midori* — This means green color. Green is abundant in plants and plants produce *Mi* (seeds). Man takes out (*toru*) *Mi* from the plant. *Mi-toru* — *Midori*.

6. *Hai-iro* — This means grey color. *Hai* means ashes. The color of ashes is grey.

7. *Shiro* and *Kuro* — White and black. White is the most yin color, and black is the most yang color. Therefore, *shiro kuro o kimeru* means yin and yang. In other words, *shiro kuro o kimeru* means decide right-wrong or give a first decision.

8. *Cha-iro* — This means brown color. *Cha* is a tea. Brown is a tea color.

9. *Sato-imo* — Albi. *Sato* means a village. *Imo* means potato. Therefore, this means a potato grown in a plain but not in a mountain. A mountain potato is called *Yamaimo*.

10. *Gen-mai* — Brown Rice. This is not of Japanese but of Chinese origin. In Japanese, *Gen Mai* means *Kuro Kome*, which means black rice. However, in this case *Kuro* does not mean black but origin, void, or a beginning of life.

Appendix 3

Sentence Patterns

Japanese sentence patterns are very simple. You must remember only a few rules. One of them is that the verb always comes at the last. I will show you Japanese sentence patterns, comparing them to English sentence patterns.

    1a. English   N - V pattern
                              I work.
        Japanese   *Watakushi wa hataraku*
                              (or *hatarakimasu.*)

WA — Many begining students of Japanese omit this particle because there is no such word in English. However, this word is very important in Japanese. WA follows the subject of the sentence. In other words, WA is an indicator of the subject of the sentence. A noun Watakushi is not a subject of the sentence. With WA, watakushi becomes the subject of the sentence above. Sometimes GA is used in place of WA. GA, however, has a specific meaning. For example:

    Watakushi ga hataraku. — I but not you work.

Notice the difference between *hataraku* and *hataraki* in the above examples. *Hataraku* is a basic form of the verb *Hatarak-u*. The last letter "U" changes to "i" in this case when the "U" is not the last letter being followed by other words such as "masu." *Hataraku* is too abrupt an expression. *Hataraki-masu* is more smooth and gentle. Therefore, *Hataraki-masu* is used commonly.

Examples of WA and GA:
Ame (rain) *wa furi-masu* (falls) — Rain Falls. Natural fact. (This sentence is saying that rain falls but not rises.)
Ame (rain) *ga furi-masu* — It is rainy. (Rain is falling but not snow or stone.)
Kaze (wind) *wa fuki-masu* (blows) — Wind blows. A natural fact. (This sentence is saying that wind blows but not falls.)
Kaze (wind) *ga fuki-masu* — It is windy. (It is the wind but not sands that are blowing now.)

    1b. English: N - V - Adv
        I work hard.
    Japanese: N - Adv - V
        Watakushi wa taihen hataraku (Hataraki-masu).

Taihen means "very much" but not "hard" exactly. However, this will be the closest expression of "hard" in this case.

Notice that adverb "hard" comes at the end of the sentence in English while the adverb "*taihen*" comes before the verb in Japanese.

Other Examples:
Pattern 1:
    English: N - V - Adv
        Flowers bloom beautifully.
    Japanese: N - Adv - V
        Hana wa utsukushiku saki-masu.

Pattern 2:
    English: N^1 - V - N^2
        He earns money.
    Japanese: N^1 - N^2 - V
        Kare wa kane wo (or o) mooke-masu.

Money is an object of verb "earns." In English, an object comes after a verb. In Japanese, however, a verb always comes at the end of a sentence. Also "*o*" (or "*wo*") should be used after the object "*kane*" so that it is understood as an object of the verb "*mooke-masu.*" *Note*:

Kara (he) *ga kane* (money) *o mooke-masu* (earn).

Other examples of pattern 2: *Anatawa* (You) *wa eigo* (English) *o hanashi-masu* (speak). Sometimes GA is used in place of O to indicate an object. *Watakushi* (I) *wa kore* (this) *ga suki-desu* (like is) means I like this but not that. *Watakushi* (I) *wa anata* (you) *ga suki-desu* means I like you, not her or them.

Pattern 3:
    English: N^1 - V - N^2 - N^2
        He gives his child a present.
    Japanese: N^1 - N^2 - N^2 - V
        Kare wa kare-no (his) *kodomo-ni okurimono o age-masu.*

        Wa — indicates the subject
        Ni — indicates a receiver of action
        (W)o — indicates an object of action

Other examples: *Watakushi wa Joonz o daitooryoo ni erabimasu* means I elect Jones president. *Note*: In Japanese the place of the receiver or object of action can be exchanged without changing any other words because *Ni* and *Wo* indicate their functions.

Pattern 4:
    English: N^1 - LV (linking verb) - N^1
        I   am   a student.
    Japanese: N^1 - N^1 - LV
        Watakushi wa seito (a student or students) *desu.* Or, *Kare wa seito desu.*

    English: N^1 - LV - Adj
        She is beautiful.
    Japanese: N^1 - Adj - LV
        Kanojo wa utsukushii (beautiful) *desu.*

In common conversation, such as this case, "*desu*" is often omitted. So we say, "*Kanojo wa utsukushii.*"

Other examples: *Anata wa byooki rashii* means You look sick.

Since *rashii* is an adjective, this sentence does not follow the rule that all sentences end with verbs. However, in this sentence the thought is not complete. The correct sentence would be *"Anata wa byooki rashii desu."* However, in common conversation, Japanese omit the verb *"desu."*

    English: N^1 - LV - adv.
        They are here.

Pattern 5: Inverted Sentence Pattern
    English: N^2 - PV (passive verb) - N^1
        A flower   is given   by him.
    Japanese: N^2 - N^1 - PV
        Hana ga kare ni yotte ataerare-masu.
        (A flower or flowers) him - by given - is.

Although this sentence is not wrong, Japanese rarely uses the passive pattern.

    English: He was elected as President.
    Japanese: *Kara wa daitooryo ni erabare-mashita.* (*"Mashita"* is
        a past form of the verb *"masu."*)

Pattern 6: Question
    English: HV (helping verb) - N^1 - V - N^2
        Do   you like this?
    Japanese: N^1 - N^2 - V - HV
        Anata wa kore ga suki-desu ka? (You this like?)

    English: Is she pretty?
    Japanese: *Kanojo wa kirei desu ka?* (She pretty is?)

Appendix 4

A Japanese Article Written in Roman Alphabet
by Torahiko Terada

Professor Terada was a famous physicist of Japan who lived in the early part of the 20th century. He was well known for his writings on scientific thoughts concerning daily living, poems, and other literary topics. He urged the use of Roman alphabets instead of Chinese characters in order to make Japanese understood by the world. Here I show you one of his articles written in Roman alphabets.

KAISUI (Ocean Water) *no KAGAKU* (chemical) *SEIBUN* (composition)
   Kaisui wa taezu (always) *Rikuchi* (land) *kara* (from) *nagarekomu* (pour in, flow in). *Mizu* (water) *de oginawarete* (be supplied) *iru kara* (since), *Rikuchi ni aru yoona* (which) *Bussitsu* (matter) *wa taitei* (almost) *mina* (all) *Kaisui ni fukumarete isoo ni omowareru ga, konnichi* (today) *madeni* (till) *Bunseki* (analyse) *no* (of) *Kekka* (result) *de miidasareta Genso* (elements) *no Kazu* (number) *wa wadukani* (only) *32 de* (is). *Sononaka de* (Within) *mottomo* (most) *ooku* (many) *fukumarete* (contained) *iru* (is) *no wa Enso* (Cl), *Syuuso* (Br), *Natoriumu* (Na), *Kariumu* (K), *Magunesiumu* (Mg) *nado* (etc.) *de aru* (are). Akagane (Copper) *ya* (and) *Nikkeru* (Ni) *nado mo Umikusa* (seaweed) *no nake* (inside) *ni aru*. *Kin* (Gold) *ya Gin* (Silver) *nado mo sukoshi* (a little) *aru*; *Umi* (Ocean) *no Midu* (water) *zentai* (totality/whole) *ni fukumareru* (contained) *Gin no Ryoo* (amount) *wa 133 — oku —* ton (13.3 billion tons) *gurai* (about)

aru to iu koto de aru (be said). *Radiumu* (Radium) *mo sukoshi* (a little) *aru; 1 guramu* (gram) *no Kaisui* (ocean water) *ni tsuki* (per) 0.25 x 10-12 gr. *guraino* (about) *wadukane* (small amount) *mono de aru. Ima* (Now) *Kaisui no omona* (important or major) *Seibun* (composition) *o Hyoo* (list) *ni shite miruto* (if the compositions be listed in a chart...)

$NaCl$ 77.8% K_2SO_4 2.5%
$MgCl$ 10.9% $CaCO_3$ 0.35%
Mg_2SO_4 4.7% $MgBr$ 0.22%

Rikuchi ni giku chikai (very near) *Tokoro* (place) *nozoite* (except), *Kaisui no Seibun* (composition) *wa, fushigina hodo* (mysteriously) *doko demo* (anywhere) *onazi* (same) *de aru* (is); *koi* (thick) *to* (and) *usui* (thin), *no Chigai* (difference) *wa aru ga* (but), *fukumarete iru Enrui* (minerals) *no tagaino* (each other) *Wariai* (ratio) *wa Sekaidyuu* (all over the World) *itteishite* (constant) *iru to ittemo yoi* (can be said that the ratio of the minerals is same all over the World). *Sorede* (Therefore), *doredemo* (any) *tada* (only) *hitotsuno* (one) *Seibun* (component), *tatoeba* (for example) *Enso* (Chlorine) *no Bunryoo* (amount) *o hakareba* (measure), *sonohokano* (the other) *Seibun no Ryoo* (Amount) *mo* (also) *wakari* (be measured), *sitagatte* (therefore) *Enrui* (minerals) *no sotai* (whole) *no Bunryoo* (amount) *ga wakari, mata* (also) *Hidyuu* (specific weight) *mo* (also) *wakaru* (find out) *no de aru.* (Also specific weight can be found or measured.) Forchhammer (person's name) *to iu Hito* (person) *no sadameta* (decide) *tokoro ni yoreba.* (According to the equation of Mr. Forchhammer.)

$$\frac{\textit{Enrui} \text{ (Mineral) } \textit{Zentai} \text{ (Whole) } \textit{no Bunryo} \text{ (Amount)}}{\textit{Enso} \text{ (Chlorine) } \textit{no Bunryo} \text{ (Amount)}} = 1.818$$

The Author

George Ohsawa was born in Kyoto, Japan, on October 18, 1883. His mother died when he was nine years old and his father disappeared. Thus, he had to take care of his younger brother and sister at the age of nine.

At the age of eighteen, Ohsawa developed intestinal and pulmonary tuberculosis. Doctors had given up on him. However, he reestablished his health by eating the diet taught by Dr. Sagen Ishizuka. Then, he vowed to teach this diet, the "Macrobiotic Medicine," to suffering peoples. He devoted his life to teaching macrobiotics until World War II.

When World War II started, he gradually involved himself in the political field and published many books against Japanese militarism, which caused him to be arrested by the Japanese Government.

In July of 1944, he predicted that Japan would be defeated, and to all of his students who were at the front, he sent telegrams which read: "You should eat carefully and be the last winner." Japan surrendered the next year. In November of 1944, he tried to reach Moscow through Manchuria in order to ask Russia to be a mediator of World War II. En route, he was chased by the military police and forced to change his plan. He escaped capture, however, and returned to Japan to plan another attempt.

On January 25, 1945, he was captured in his hideout and jailed under conditions in which the temperature went as low as twenty degrees below zero (centigrade). After three months of such treatment, he became extremely weak, lost eighty percent of his eyesight, and almost died.

At the end of June, he was suddenly released with the stipulation that he would not bring a law suit against the government.

In July, he attempted a coup d'etat with Generals Iimori and Fujimori, but was captured again at a secret meeting, jailed in Kofu, and subsequently transferred to a prison in Nagasaki. Kofu was bombed completely after he was moved. In August, Japan surrendered. In September, he was released by the order of General MacArthur, just before the date set for his execution. He wrote a letter appealing to MacArthur, advising him to diminish the military and secret police of the Japanese government. The advice was taken, and those systems were abolished.

After the war, Ohsawa devoted himself to the education of young Japanese instead of curing the sick. About twenty students out of thousands went to Europe, America, India, and South America. They later established macrobiotic centers in many countries.

He left Japan to teach macrobiotics to the world. After lecture tours in India, Africa, Belgium, Switzerland, Germany, Sweden, Italy, England, and France, he came to the United States in December 1959.

In 1960, he published the book *Zen Macrobiotics*. It sold almost a quarter of a million copies and is still selling well. Also, a macrobiotic magazine called *Macrobiotic News* was published by his disciple Herman Aihara. Now titled *Macrobiotics Today,* it is published by the George Ohsawa Macrobiotic Foundation in Chico, California.

Ohsawa's macrobiotic diet was a forerunner of today's natural living and organic food trends, because he warned against chemicals in foods and in cultivation.

A list of books by George Ohsawa and others on macrobiotics can be obtained from the George Ohsawa Macrobiotic Foundation, PO Box 3998, Chico, CA 95927-3998; 530-566-9765; fax 530-566-9768; *gomf@earthlink.net.* Or, visit *www.OhsawaMacrobiotics.com.*

www.ingramcontent.com/pod-product-compliance
Lightning Source LLC
Chambersburg PA
CBHW020023050426
42450CB00005B/614